CONSERVATION 2000

Rain Forests

First Published 1992

© Joy A. Palmer 1992

Typeset by J&L Composition Ltd, Filey, North Yorkshire
and printed in Hong Kong
by Colorcraft Ltd

Published by
B.T. Batsford Ltd
4 Fitzhardinge Street
London W1H 0AH

A CIP catalogue record for this book is available from the British Library

ISBN 0 7134 6573 5

Acknowledgements

The Author and Publishers would like to thank the following for permission to reproduce illustrations:
FAO for page 42; Hutchison Library for pages 43 and 52; Premaphotos Wildlife for page 53; Science Photo Library for pages 10, 36 and 41; Frank Spooner Pictures for page 59; Zefa for pages 28 and 29. The illustrations on pages 6/7, 10/11, 14/15, 18, 19, 22, 23, 24, 26/27, 30, 31, 32, 34, 38, 40, 44, 45, 46, 48, 49, 51, 54, 55, 56, 57 and 59 were supplied by the Author. The Author would also like to thank Commander J. Scullion of SKS/Simmah Timber Industries. The diagrams on pages 8, 9, 12, 13, 20, 21, 36, 37, 45, 49 and 53 were drawn by Ken Smith.

CONSERVATION 2000

Rain Forests

Joy Palmer

B.T. Batsford Ltd · London

CONTENTS

INTRODUCTION

Tropical rainforests are some of the most beautiful and important places on our earth. They are also some of the most complex. The mention of the word forest immediately causes most people to think of trees – and, indeed, trees are the central component of rainforest life. Yet the forests are far more than a collection of trees. They sustain native people. They provide a habitat for countless millions of plants, animals, birds and insects. They supply so much that the world takes for granted – fruits, vegetables, spices, nuts, medicines, oils, rubber and innumerable other goods as well as timber. They also supply information for scientists and researchers, so helping advancements in the worlds of agriculture, industry and medicine.

The forests have a number of interdependent elements, including animal and plant life, people, soils, water and air. Together, these elements make up a fascinating and complex ecosystem. All of the elements need each other. Furthermore, the rainforests as a whole are one key element of our planet Earth. Together with other features such as oceans, deserts and grasslands, they make up a balanced natural world or global ecosystem. If rainforests are disturbed or disappear, then the world as a whole will be affected in dramatic and highly complex ways.

This book begins by stressing the great beauty and values of the world's tropical forests. It looks at their key features, their climate, and each of the component ele-

ments. The problematic issues are then addressed – the rate of deforestation and the complex and multiple causes of this, both direct and indirect. Problems lead to inevitable consequences and, again, the complex and inter-related aspects of these are discussed.

Finally, the book looks at positive action that is being taken, and ways in which this might be extended at a range of levels from individual to international.

In many ways, rainforests may seem very remote from our own lives. Yet it is hoped that the following pages will provide knowledge and understanding of their complexities, and that these FACTS will lead to ACTION.

WHAT & WHERE ARE TROPICAL RAINFORESTS?

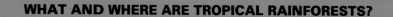

A tropical rainforest – a place of outstanding beauty. These forests contain more than half of the world's plant and animal species

Every layer in the forest is vital. Long-established trees and ground level plants are all important habitats for animal, bird and insect life

Some parts of planet Earth are covered with vast areas of ever-green forest land which receive very large amounts of rainfall. These places are known as tropical rainforests. At least 400 centimetres of rain falls on them each year. The trees in such a forest are so close together that their branches touch one another – they form a 'closed canopy', allowing very little light to reach the ground.

Rainforests lie in a huge belt, north and south of the equator. These are called the equatorial areas of the world, between the Tropic of Cancer and the Tropic of Capricorn. Originally the area of the world covered by these forests was much larger than it is today. Many forests have been cut down and others continue to disappear.

The Current Extent of Tropical Rainforests

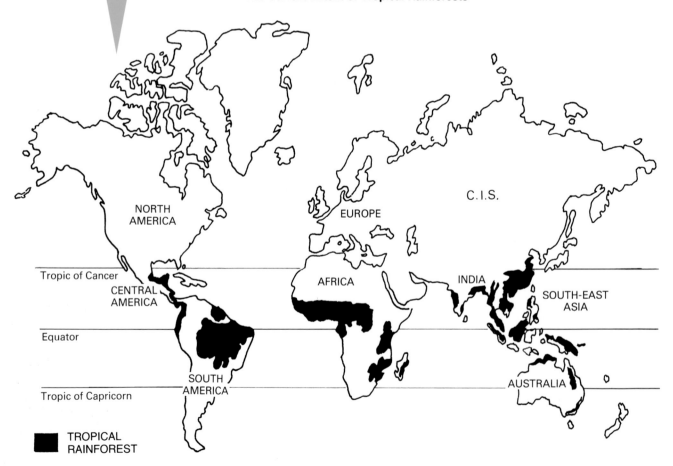

TROPICAL
RAINFOREST

Once, the earth had an estimated 1.5 billion hectares of tropical rainforests. This is only three per cent of the planet's total area, but for many reasons that will become apparent in the following pages, it was a crucial three per cent in terms of the ecology of our earth. Today only 900 million hectares remain. Some estimate the rate of loss at 11 million hectares every year although estimates do vary. The forests that remain are located in three large blocks: the Congo basin in the western part of Central Africa, the Amazon basin in South America, and the Malay Archipelago which is between Australia and South-East Asia.

No two rainforests are the same as far as their appearance is concerned. A wide variety of trees and plants grow in a range of shapes and sizes. One hectare of rainforest may have, for example, between one and two hundred tree species. It is possible that only a single tree from a particular

species will be found in an area that size. Other varieties of plants are present in amazing quantities – 7,000 types of flowering plants have been identified in West African forests, 40,000 in Brazil and an incredible 13,000 on the island of Madagascar.

Despite this diversity of tree and plant types, tropical forests do have certain features of 'shape' or growth in common. All mature forests that have been established for a large number of years are called primary forests, and they can be seen to have a number of layers making up a total structure known as a **gallery.** Each layer within this gallery will have its own range of species of trees or other plants.

The **canopy** is a dense uninterrupted layer of tree tops, some 40 metres above the ground. Trees making up this layer have thin trunks with branches only at the very top. These trees act as an umbrella to both rainfall and

Every layer of the rainforest is vital. The forest must be interpreted as a unified structure in which everything is interrelated, and each element has an essential role to play in the survival of the ecosystem as a whole. If disappearing rainforests are to be saved, then every layer must be conserved.

sunshine – little can reach the ground. Indeed, beneath the canopy it is dark and gloomy. A layer known as a **sub-canopy** has trees which struggle for light, sheltering in their turn long-leaved plants, ferns and young trees. Above the canopy rise the majestic **emergents** – a smaller number of 50 metre tall trees with long, thin trunks which stretch their crowns into the air above all else. Each hectare of land will have only one or two of these great giants.

CLIMATE & SOILS OF THE FORESTS

The climate of tropical rainforests may be summed up in two key words: HOT and WET. They are hot all year round, with very little variation in temperature from month to month or from day to night. For example, in the Brazilian rainforest, the average maximum temperature varies only from 30°C to 32°C throughout the year, and the average minimum from 22°C to 23°C. This consistency is particularly noticeable below the forest canopy where temperatures are more constant than in any other ecosystem on our planet. An important point to bear in mind is that this affects animal and plant life. All living things in the forests are used to this constant heat, so if there is any significant change, they find it very difficult to adapt. When parts of a forest are removed, this inevitably leads to wider ranges in temperature. Without the canopy acting as a sun shade, it will become hotter during the day and cooler at night. Also, more moisture will be lost through the process of evaporation. This will have the serious effect of changing conditions for plant and animal life.

Whilst rainforests are always wet, there is much greater variation in daily and monthly patterns of rainfall than there is in temperature. It does not rain every

Trees of the hot, wet forest keep their leaves all through the year. The forest may appear from a distance to be dull patches of green, yet within and below the canopy is a complex web of colourful and fascinating life

day of the year. In most areas, the majority of the rainfall occurs in a series of incredibly heavy storms. In some places there are quite large variations throughout the year. Some months may have well over 300 mm of rain and others only 180 mm. Perhaps the word 'only' should not be used, for this is still a very large quantity of rain compared with figures for many other parts of the world. Rain forests are indeed very wet and 'thirsty' places, needing at least 100 mm of rain a month in order to thrive. If the level falls below this, then trees and plants will use up reserves of water from within the ground. There is no way that the plants and the animals of the forests would survive with constant shortages of water.

Once again, there is a link between the problems of rain forest destruction and climate. These torrential downpours of rain can be 'caught' and absorbed by the mass of trees and plants. This dense vegetation is rather like an umbrella which protects the surface of the earth. If this umbrella is removed, the results are dramatic – rain hits the ground with tremendous force, soil is washed away removing vital supplies of nutrients for the plants, and there is a great likelihood of flooding. Sometimes, parts of a forest are cleared so that crops can be grown for food. If flooding has occurred the soil that remains is of little use for growing crops: that which has been washed away causes rivers to be blocked up with silt, thus contributing to extensive flooding.

Rainforests are therefore very important in terms of their contribution to agriculture and to weather patterns. Because rainfall

The Daily Rhythm in a Tropical Forest . . .

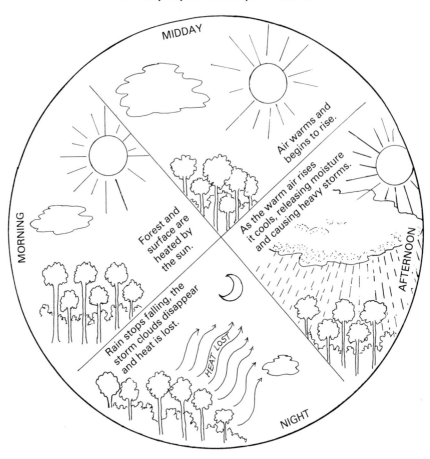

is reliable in a stable forest, people can depend on it to water their crops. Destruction of forests means loss of irrigation for agriculture. It also means destruction of rainfall cycles. Together with the build-up of the gas carbon dioxide in the earth's atmosphere which results from removing forests, this problem also contributes to the 'Greenhouse Effect' which is a general warming of the earth's atmosphere, a phenomenon which has the potential for devastating effects on our planet.

Rainforest soils are actually very poor at storing the nutrients which plants need for food. Organic nutrients, or those which come from plants and animals through the process of decomposition, are taken up out of the soil in enormous quantities be-

cause there are so many plants to absorb them. Plant nutrients move through the decomposition cycle far more rapidly in a rainforest environment than they do in other ecosystems. The result of this is that very few nutrients are stored in the soil. There is also a very poor store of mineral nutrients from the rocks underneath the soil: the minerals are soluble in water, and rain passing through the soil washes them away in a process known as leaching.

It seems very curious that the soils of the forests are so poor or infertile, when they support such a wealth and diversity of plant life. As most of the nutrients are stored within this plant life rather than the soil, the effects of removing the trees are obvious and the consequences are very serious.

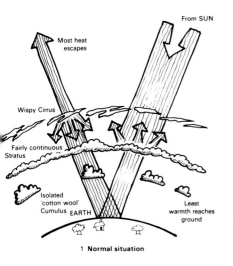

1 **Normal situation**

2 **In-between condition**

3 **Full Greenhouse Effect**

Trees take in or absorb carbon dioxide from the atmosphere (we breathe this *out*) and give off oxygen (we breathe this *in*). When trees are removed, a lot of carbon dioxide will be left in the air. This traps heat in the atmosphere rather like glass traps heat in a greenhouse. The result is called 'the Greehouse Effect'. Gradually the earth warms up and temperatures rise all over the world. This phenomenon is called global warming

The Cycle of Decomposition

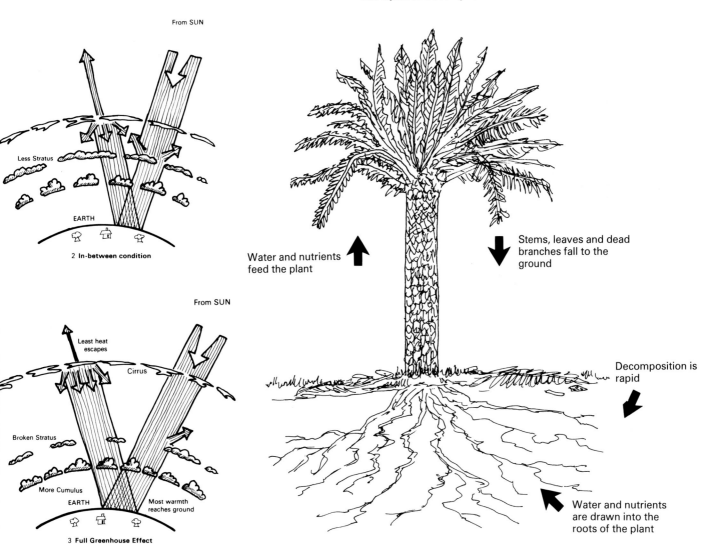

Water and nutrients feed the plant

Stems, leaves and dead branches fall to the ground

Decomposition is rapid

Water and nutrients are drawn into the roots of the plant

Tapir (left), parrot (top), monkey (above) and green-winged butterfly (background); some of the incredibly varied range of creatures to be found in the rainforest

So much of the value of tropical rainforests lies in their sheer beauty and diversity of life. They are dramatically exciting and colourful places, providing a home for one half of all the plant and animal species in the world. The range and diversity of plant life has already been considered, and this vegetation feeds and provides shelter for huge numbers of insects, birds and larger animals. As with the plants, the fascination is with the quantity and variety of animal species rather than the great numbers of any one type. The only creatures present in colossal numbers are invertebrates – the tiny animals without backbones. There are millions of ants and termites and thousands of species of beautiful tropical butterflies. It is estimated that a small patch of forest 6 km square may house some 40,000 species of insects. Because the forest floor is covered with dead leaves and decomposing vegetation, it will provide food and shelter for countless other invertebrate creatures such as ants, beetles, snails, spiders and millipedes. In turn, these will provide food for larger species such as frogs, snakes, lizards, mammals and birds.

Amphibians and reptiles are colourful and fascinating members of the forest community. Many have adapted to forest life by developing ways of climbing and 'flying'. Some frogs lay their eggs on leaves and can travel from tree to tree by using their large webbed toes as parachutes. A 'flying' snake curls its flattened body into a coil and glides through the air from one tree to another. It may live high up in the canopy, camouflaged amongst the leaves.

The canopy is also the home of

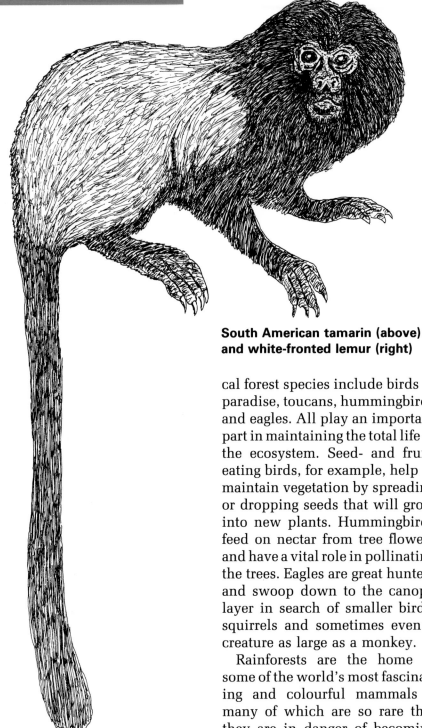

South American tamarin (above) and white-fronted lemur (right)

many species of birds. The 6 km square patch may be home to some 400 varieties, attracted by the endless supply of seeds and tree fruits. Macaws and other members of the parrot family are common in South American forests. Other well-known tropi-

cal forest species include birds of paradise, toucans, hummingbirds and eagles. All play an important part in maintaining the total life of the ecosystem. Seed- and fruit-eating birds, for example, help to maintain vegetation by spreading or dropping seeds that will grow into new plants. Hummingbirds feed on nectar from tree flowers and have a vital role in pollinating the trees. Eagles are great hunters and swoop down to the canopy layer in search of smaller birds, squirrels and sometimes even a creature as large as a monkey.

Rainforests are the home of some of the world's most fascinating and colourful mammals — many of which are so rare that they are in danger of becoming extinct. African forests are well-known for being the home of gorillas. These large primates are too heavy to live in the trees and spend their time on the ground in search of food. They have huge appetites for vegetation, so travel quite long distances each day to find a range of suitable food. The

Key issues for conservation

Many species are rare and in danger of extinction.
It is estimated, for example, that less than 100 golden lion tamarins still exist, and an even smaller number of cotton top tamarins.

Many creatures spend their entire lives in just one layer of the forest.
Each of the three key layers has its own group of residents, with the canopy being the most densely populated.

Many creatures are highly specialized and linked to a particular niche.
Certain monkeys, for example, will only eat the fruits from one type of tree; sloths are adapted to hang upside down, suspended from branches.

Therefore:
THE WHOLE STRUCTURE OF THE FOREST MUST BE CONSERVED.

gorilla population is certainly threatened with extinction and new measures must be taken in order to protect them.

Lemurs, sloths, squirrels and bats are amongst the many other mammals which live high up amongst the forest trees. Few varieties spend their life at surface level because of its lack of light and scarcity of vegetation. The forests of the Amazon and of South-East Asia have tapirs, and a number of areas have representatives of the cat family including the morgay and the jaguar.

ADAPTATION, RENEWAL, FRAGILITY

The Good: Adaptation to very special and complex circumstances

The Bad: Interdependence and Sensitivity = Fragility

Before the value of the rainforests is explored in greater depth, three further, and related features of the forest ecosystem must be considered. The first of these is the concept of **adaptation.** This means the way living things change their form and way of life to suit their environmental conditions. The trees of a rainforest are highly adapted so that they thrive in their very special conditions.

A long-necked fowl demonstrates the effectiveness of camouflage

For example, the root systems develop much nearer to the surface of the ground than they would normally. This is because water and limited nutrient supplies are usually within a metre of the surface. Because the roots do not penetrate deep into the soil and the trees are so heavy, there is a danger that they could fall over. Again, adaptation has resulted in the growth of enormous buttresses or solid roots on the bottom portion of the trunks, which give support to the trees.

Another example of tree adaptation is the way leaves adapt to where they are in relation to sunlight. Sunlight is essential for all trees as it helps the leaves to make the foods necessary for plants through the process of photosynthesis. For this reason, a good number of the leaves of each plant must receive some light from the sun, so there is intense competition. Below the canopy where sunlight fails to penetrate, leaves grow very large so that they have a better chance of catching the light. At the top of the canopy, light is plentiful, so leaves tend to be much smaller. All leaves grow at an angle so that they face the sunlight.

Animals, too, have developed special adaptation techniques for rainforest life — such as the example of the amphibians and reptiles which succeed in travelling from tree to tree at canopy level. Because of such adaptations, and the special conditions needed by many species, all life in the forest is sensitive to change. Removing only a small number of trees, for example, exposes the buttresses of others to storms and they may well blow down.

A second key feature is **renewal.**

Leaf Adaptations by Rainforest Plants

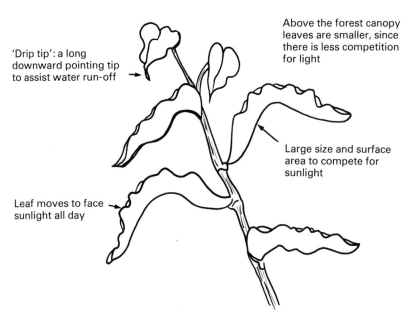

'Drip tip': a long downward pointing tip to assist water run-off

Above the forest canopy leaves are smaller, since there is less competition for light

Large size and surface area to compete for sunlight

Leaf moves to face sunlight all day

A rainforest tree may live for up to 500 years but, like all living things, must eventually die. Replacement is essential in order to preserve the structure of the forest as a whole. Forests naturally renew themselves through a process of succession. This involves various stages of natural plant growth. Any scheme aimed at conservation of forests should follow this natural pattern. When gaps appear in the canopy it is important that there are enough seeds of the correct type available at the appropriate stage. If the aim is to regrow a forest in a cleared area, then this natural succession can be imitated by planting the right seeds at the right time.

A third key concept is **fragility.** This may seem an odd word to describe a huge and mighty forest, but in this context, it means that rainforests are not at all good at coping with or recovering from disturbance. They are in fact one of the most fragile ecosystems on our planet. Reasons for fragility are related to other key ideas, including adaptation — the trees, animals and soils have had thousands of years to adapt to very special, complex and interrelated conditions. This makes them very vulnerable to change. Most have lived in remarkably unchanging conditions for a very long time.

Other reasons for fragility include the fact that most of the food is stored in the vegetation and little is available in the soil; also, there may be only one or two members of a particular tree species in a patch of forest. Tree seeds do not spread easily, and may fail to germinate, so natural renewal may not take place. Thus all of the interdependent elements of the forest are very sensitive to change. Furthermore, because of this characteristic of interdependence and the 'wholeness' of the forest, if there is a change in any element it will inevitably have a far-reaching effect on many other aspects of the ecosystem.

Three Stage Succession In Forest Renewal

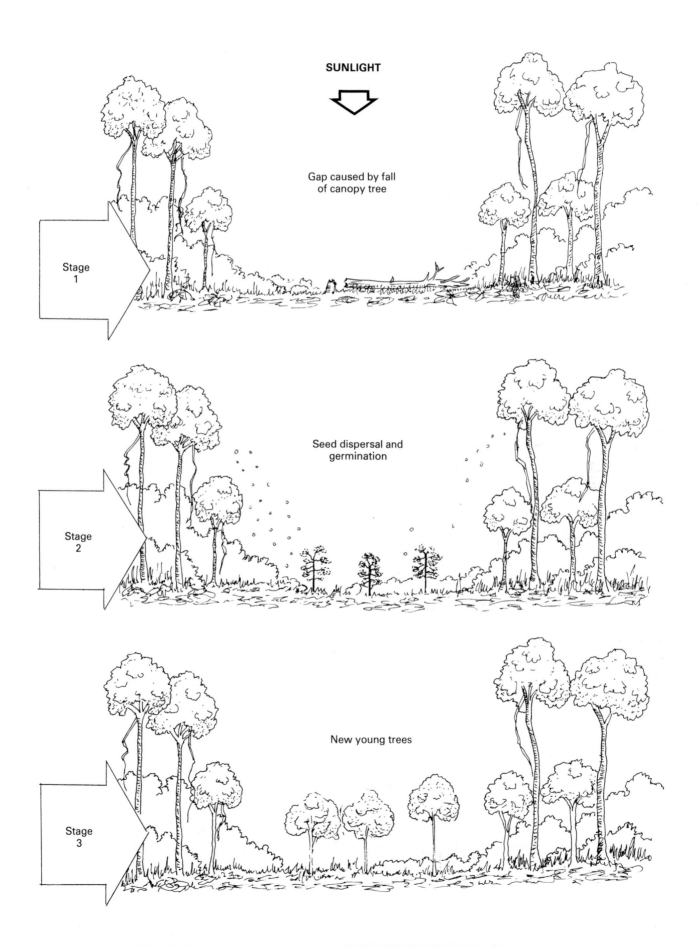

SUNLIGHT

Gap caused by fall
of canopy tree

Stage
1

Seed dispersal and
germination

Stage
2

New young trees

Stage
3

FORESTS OF VALUE: TIMBER, FOOD & MEDICINES

The chief components of tropical rainforests, namely the trees, are seen to be a valuable source of revenue and timber by many nations of the world. Highly-prized woods found in forests include teak, mahogany and rose-wood. These are species of hard-wood trees which have a very high commercial value. Teak and mahogany, for example, are woods that last for hundreds of years, and are much in demand for the manufacture of such things as good quality furniture and boats. Demand for hardwood by the industrial nations of the world, including the United Kingdom and the USA, has risen dramatic-ally in the past 40 years.

Terraced vegetable gardens have been established in the forests of Malaysia

Tropical forests for our well-being

malaria
Treated with quinine from the cinchona tree of Peru.

surgery
Relies on d-turbocuranine – a substance which relaxes muscles – made from curare, derived from an Amazonian liana.

birth control
A major component of the contraceptive pill is diosgenin from Mexican and Guatemalan wild yams.

dental cement
Comes from balsams of Latin America.

glaucoma eye disease
Is treated with diosgenin from the West African calabar bean.

antiseptic
Can be obtained from a Malaysian benzoin tree. This is also effective in the treatment of bronchitis.

Not only do tropical countries have the timber, they also have the added attraction of low labour costs. Furthermore, the sale of timber provides immediate benefits for those in a position to supply it. For many developing nations, exports of hardwood timbers are a major source of income. Between 1975 and 1990 annual income from these exports averaged at around £4.8 billion. In addition, tropical nations themselves also use large quantities of wood for fuel.

Important as timber clearly is, it is only one of a number of goods and products that tropical forests supply, and which we take for granted. They also provide fruits, vegetables, spices, nuts, medicines, oils, rubber and many other industrial goods.

The forests support an incredible diversity of edible plants which provide food for people throughout the world, as well as the inhabitants of tropical lands. Wild varieties of grains such as wheat, corn, rice and millet are all found in the tropics. A seemingly endless list of fruits, nuts and vegetables grow there, including bananas, pineapples, yams, coffee and sugar-cane. Part of the excitement of agriculture in these lands is the potential for new discoveries in terms of edible items. Once again, the sale of these goods provides valuable revenue for exporting countries.

Related to this discussion on food crops is the less obvious 'product' of the advancement of techniques for controlling disease and pests. Many common food plants originated in the tropical forests and have related wild species growing there. These are highly valuable from the point of

view of having genetic materials that can be used to alter or 'modify' crops throughout the world in order to produce new varieties that resist pests and diseases. For example, wild tropical varieties of rice have been used to aid the development of an Asian rice that is protected from four major diseases. Barley in California and sugar cane in south-east USA have also been modified in this way with the help of wild varieties from trop-

ical rainforest areas.

Every year, up to 40 per cent of the world's crops are destroyed by pests. This figure could be greatly reduced by using natural pest controls from tropical forests. Such natural pesticides include three products that can be obtained from tropical plants, namely pyrethrum, rotenone and methyl carbamate. Rainforest insects are also wonderful pest controllers, since they may attack and eat eggs, larvae or even the adults of

other species. In Florida, USA, for example, three kinds of tropical parasites are imported which kill the pests of citrus fruit trees.

A very wide range of medicines derive from tropical plants and trees, and as with foods, new ones are regularly being identified by scientists and put to good use. It is estimated that one-quarter of all medical substances originally derived from plants in the tropics. Furthermore, over 1,000 plants there may contain potential cancer-fighting drugs. A leading researcher in Glasgow, Scotland, for example, discovered in 1989 that a piece of bark from a rain forest tree in the Korup National Park in Cameroon, West Africa, contained a chemical which can kill cancer cells. Research continues to see whether this chemical can be turned into a medicine and used to treat cancer patients successfully.

The chemical resources of forest trees certainly give hope for the future, and not just because of their potential life-saving possibilities. If advances in science and medicine mean that such chemicals can be removed and used to save lives, then this will result in a situation where the trees which donate them are actually more valuable in the forest than being cut down for timber, especially if profits are shared with the local people. This would be a wonderful step forward in the conservation process.

Unfortunately, tropical trees are regarded as a valuable source of income. This young teak tree growing on the edge of the forest will have high value for use in making furniture

FORESTS OF VALUE:
INDUSTRY & ENVIRONMENT

For many people, the most important feature and value of the rainforests is their incredible beauty. The rich diversity of life, the colour and the beauty have been the subject of books, films and photographs that have given pleasure to millions of people throughout the world who are not fortunate enough to be able to visit these lands and experience their aesthetic qualities personally. Rainforests create in many people a sense of wonder, of fascination and of awe. Efforts to spread this awareness of their beauty through films and other visual materials are perhaps very important from the point of view of conservation. Controlled tourism is increasing in tropical areas, bringing not only added revenue

Many people believe that the greatest value of all lies in the sheer beauty and fascination of the forest . . .

but also weight to the argument that rainforests should be preserved in their wild and beautiful natural form.

But the forests have other commercial values. As well as their vast output of timber, agricultural products and medicinal substances, tropical rainforests supply many of the products used in industry, including gums, latexes, resins, waxes, rubber, fibres, dyes, tanning substances, lubricants, oils, turpentine, rattan and bamboo.

Many of these tropical forest products are used to meet the needs of local people and so do not have economic value. Nevertheless, the value of industrial products yielded by tropical forests amounts to billions of pounds each year. Rubber is one of the most important products sold in the world economy. Rubber trees in South-East Asia are a major 'cash crop'. Natural rubber is the fourth largest agricultural export from the tropical world. Rattan is a spiky climbing plant that can be used to make a wide variety of goods, including furniture. The rattan industry of Indonesia produces around £3 million in trade each year.

Forest materials can be used to make a huge range of goods that we may buy regularly, including glue for postage stamps, golf balls, nail varnish, chewing gum, toothpaste, deodorant, shampoo, mascara, lipstick and wickerwork chairs. Some of these goods are produced without damaging rain forests. Others bring about great destruction. Conservationists are keen to promote the sale of items of the kind which have *not* necessitated the removal of valuable trees and plants.

Quite apart from goods and products which can be counted and valued, the tropical forests of our world provide essential services, not only for their local surroundings but for the earth as

. . . yet that beauty and fascination can easily turn into ugly devastation

a whole. Some of these have already been mentioned, yet they are so crucial that it is perhaps useful to provide a summary or overview of these critical features – they really do lie at the very heart of any discussion on the total *value* of tropical forests.

Firstly, the forests affect climate and the atmosphere. They alter or moderate the temperature of the air, maintain a natural water (hydrological) cycle by absorbing rainfall and then releasing moisture into the atmosphere, and they take in carbon dioxide and give out oxygen through the process known as photosynthesis.

Secondly, tropical forests have an important role to play in the shaping of the earth. They recycle organic wastes and nutrients in a very speedy and efficient way; and because the dense vegetation (especially the canopy) prevents the rainfall from battering the ground with great force, the forests control the erosion of soil, the silting up of rivers and waterways and the spread of floods.

For similar reasons, the forests also prevent, or certainly limit, rockfalls and landslides which may occur during particularly severe rainstorms or earthquakes, and they reduce potential damage from tropical cyclones. Obviously, if forests are removed, all of these hazards will have far more serious effects upon the environment. In many ways, the trees provide an 'environment protection service.'

A forest's services to the environment

climate and atmosphere
- moderates air temperatures
- maintains hydrological cycle
- takes in CO_2 and generates O_2

shaping the earth
- recycles organic nutrients and wastes
- controls soil erosion, silting of rivers, flooding
- reduces rockfalls and landslides

FORESTS OF VALUE: PEOPLE

Yanomami Indian hunting in Venezuela

Before looking more closely at the complex problem of forest destruction, one vital element of the value of the forest environment must be included – forests are homes for PEOPLE. Millions of people live in these lands, each with their own special and unique culture. Over thousands of years, such societies have acquired incredibly wide-ranging knowledge about the forest and how to use its resources wisely. Many generations have successfully found and developed ways of using local materials to build their homes, growing crops, and using the wild plants for food and medicines. One of the great tragedies of forest destruction is the fact that indigenous societies are being moved, and their numbers are declining. If forests disappear, then so will the ways of life which depend upon the forest environment. Moreover, the valuable local knowledge which these people have will be lost to the world forever.

The population of the rainforests in 1992 is estimated at about 200 million and comprises many different tribes: for example, in the African rainforests are Bushmen and pygmies; American Indian tribes inhabit the forests of South America; and in South-East Asia are found pygmies (in the Philippines), Sianh Daya people (Borneo) and Biami and Gibusi peoples (in New Guinea).

Rainforest people are essentially 'uninterrupted' cultures: that is, they have developed very distinctive ways of living which have not been subject to the same dramatic changes in lifestyle as those that have affected the world's industrial nations. Each individual tribe has its own special customs, traditions and beliefs, though many aspects of life are common to all. Traditionally, these people collected seeds and other plant food and hunted wild animals in order to feed themselves. Small areas of land are now cleared so that they can grow food crops near to their homes.

The Baka pygmies in the southeast of Cameroon in Africa make typical huts for shelter out of banana fronds. They hunt with spears crafted from nearby plants, and grow wild forms of cereals that are so much more resistant to pests and disease than crop relatives in other lands.

In the Amazonian forest of South America live the Yanomami Indians. Sometimes known as the 'fierce people', they can be very aggressive to outsiders and other tribes, whilst living closely in tune with the environment. Their approach to the natural world, like that of all forest people, is in harmony with nature: that is, they do not exploit their environment and its resources. They live, for example, in small and widely-spaced communities so that they do not make too many demands for food and resources on one patch of forest. Their buildings, made of wood and palm fronds, quickly deteriorate, and after about two years, they are left to rot, and the people move on.

Rainforest people are probably the only societies left in the world who live on our earth without destroying it. The 'great' industrial nations have grown further and further away from the natural world as they have made significant advances in science and technology, and have tried to 'master' it. Forest people on the other hand, have grown closer to nature in order to survive. In many ways this is related to the cultures, beliefs and taboos of these people, which is a fascinating area for further reading and study. They harvest an incredible wealth of foods and medicines from plants very carefully, so that the plants are not over-exploited or destroyed altogether. The Yanomami Indians, for example, gather drugs from the forest which they use to treat both mental and physical illness. These are removed with great care, and no damage is done to the ecosystem. They may clear small tracts in the trees so that crops may be grown and shelters sited, but these will be thoughtfully laid out and no lasting damage will be done.

The chief aim of the forest people is to preserve the environment in which they live. The forest is their entire world and they see themselves, quite rightly, as being an interrelated part of the total environment.

Sadly, the number of people in certain tribes in tropical rain forests is gradually declining – a tragedy for traditional cultures and societies. As forests are removed, people are displaced and traditions inevitably destroyed.

Colombian rainforest inhabitants preparing food

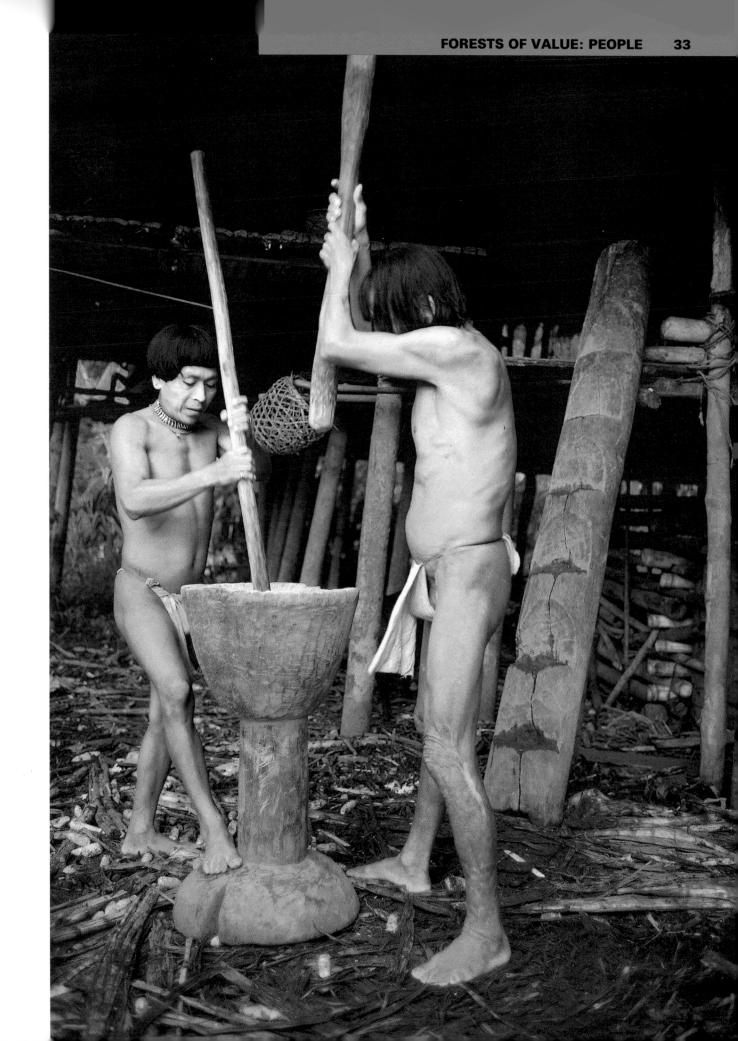

DEFORESTATION: RATES & CAUSES

Deforestation results from a number of direct and indirect causes including agriculture, logging, mining and large-scale developments such as housing, road and rail construction

Some causes of deforestation

Area	Causes
Brazil (Rondonia Province)	Government policy encouraging colonization
Columbia, Ecuador	Commercial logging, shifting cultivation
Ivory Coast, Ghana, Sierra Leone	Shifting cultivation, fuelwood needs, commercial logging
Madagascar	Shifting cultivation, cattle grazing, charcoal production
Malaysia	Agricultural development, commercial logging, large-scale plantations
Philippines	Shifting cultivation, logging
Papua New Guinea	Mining
South-west India	Shifting cultivation, fuelwood needs

The destruction (or deforestation) of tropical rainforests is taking place at an alarming rate. Once they covered an area almost twice the size of the USA – around 1.5 billion hectares: today less than 900 million hectares remain, and every day that figure is reduced. These statistics include evergreen tropical forests, but not deciduous or semi-deciduous moist tropical forests. Figures on destruction rates are rather complex – they depend on which types of tropical forest are included, and what level of disturbance of a forest is actually defined as deforestation or forest clearing.

A survey by the United Nations Food and Agriculture Organisation estimates that about 7.5 million hectares of closed tropical forest – 0.6 per cent of the world's total – disappear every year. The World Wide Fund for Nature (WWF) thinks that a figure such as this dramatically underestimates the damage that is being done to forests. The United Nations survey does not, for example, take account of excessive grazing by animals, accidental damage from fire or gathering of firewood. The WWF estimates the true rate of destruction at 1.15 per cent of the world's total per year. The UN claims that '. . . at the present rate of destruction, all accessible tropical rainforests will have disappeared by the end of this century.'

Recent data gained by satellite showed that in 1989 some 8 million hectares of forest land

may have been burned in Brazil alone. These data certainly support the UN's chilling prediction.

Deforestation rates are not the same across the world and vary according to region, local conditions and the relative impact of various causes of forest destruction. Africa as a whole lost 23 per cent of its moist tropical forest in a period of 30 years; in the 1980s, more than 5 per cent of the moist coastal forests of West Africa were being cleared each year. The Ivory Coast has lost 66 per cent of its forests in the last 25 years. Perhaps the most alarming statistic is from Latin America – 99 per cent of Brazil's Atlantic coast moist forest has been removed.

So the two serious questions to be addressed are clearly – WHY are rainforests being destroyed at such an alarming rate? And WHAT is the world able to do about this? The causes of deforestation are multiple and com-

plex. The chief direct causes are agriculture, logging for timber and industry, cattle ranching, industrial activities such as mining, and large-scale development projects. Interlinked with these is another range of more indirect causes, including human population growth, ever-increasing demands throughout the world for forest products, unequal distribution of territory in the tropical lands, poverty, and finally world economics – the developing world has a great and increasing financial debt to pay.

Underpinning many of these causes (some of which will be considered in closer detail on the following pages) are the immediate needs of the people who live in tropical lands. Many forests are cut in order to provide immediate benefits. The forests are seen to have no obvious value if left standing, but when cut down and

Cutting a log at a sawmill

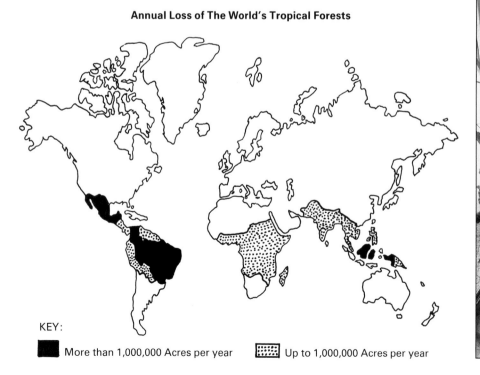

Annual Loss of The World's Tropical Forests

KEY:

█ More than 1,000,000 Acres per year   ▦ Up to 1,000,000 Acres per year

Rainforest Homes Use Up Timber

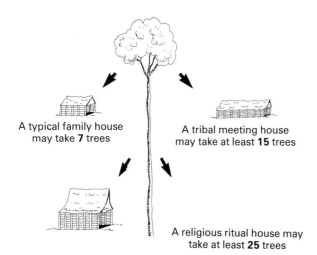

A typical family house may take **7** trees

A tribal meeting house may take at least **15** trees

A religious ritual house may take at least **25** trees

tracts of forest to be cleared or disturbed.

To the threats from within must be added major direct threats from outside the forest. Trees mean wealth. They represent many products that fetch high prices in the richer industrial nations of the world. It is not really surprising that international industries, companies and governments should support schemes to remove timber, agricultural and industrial products.

cleared they give space for valuable farmland, and the sale of the timber provides desperately needed income for the nation.

Another way of dividing up and analysing the complex causes of deforestation is to understand which of these causes come from within the forests and which from outside. One of the most significant of those from within is human population growth. Providing the forests are not taken away from local people, one village may double its population within the next 25 years, especially if hygiene and health care continue to improve. In addition, in some countries the government encourages migration from urban to rural areas to reduce the pressures of over-population of the cities.

In order to accommodate this huge increase – to have space for shelter, to grow enough food – more and more forest will need to be cleared. The boundaries of the village will be pushed further and further into the forest. It may even be decided to establish a new village. On a worldwide scale, the population explosion will mean millions of extra people to be housed and fed – causing vast

---

Timber Trades Journal
10 February 1990

First 'green' timber importer sets up shop

A new timber importer is set to distribute its first batch of sustainably-sourced timber in the UK. Newcastle-upon-Tyne-based *Ecological Trading Company* takes delivery on February 28 of its first shipment of sustainably-sourced hardwood from Peru and is looking for merchants willing to stock the wood. So far the company has only signed-up one merchant, *Milland Fine Timber*, near Liphook, Hampshire.

The shipment, the first since the company was set-up last year, will be supplied with a 'sustainability guarantee', along with a description of its production methods.

ETC claims that the timber trade is partly responsible for the destruction of the rainforests but that it has the potential to become part of the solution. The company says that it is going to demonstrate this.

Existing importers, it says, only have tenuous links with their sources because 'most buying is done through agents', whereas ETC deals directly with producers, maintaining close relations with them. ETC asserts that traditional timber importers buy from 'wherever they can: price, quality and appearance are the only criteria', it says.

Higher hardwood prices is a direct result of the company's sustainable-sourcing. Hubert Kwisthout, director of ETC, admits that it intends to pay producers 'substantially' higher prices for their timber.

He added that the company's effort to source sustainable timber has been difficult, though.

'We are trying to find as much tropical timber as possible, but it is complicated: a number of countries claim that they have sustainable production, but we're looking at development that involves the local inhabitants – a whole different approach which will bring long-term benefits.'

Reprinted courtesy of the *Timber Trades Journal*.

Rainforests – sustainable timber harvesting

A Co-operative in the Palcazu Valley, in Peru, has been pioneering techniques for managing the natural forest, rather than clear felling and replacing the forest with a mono-culture plantation. Elsewhere in the tropics destructive forestry techniques are decimating the bio-diversity of these extraordinarily rich regions. In projects like the one in the Palcazu Valley an example is being shown of a way forward out of the current madness of so much of the tropical timber trade – but will the trade take note?

The co-operative is run by the local Yanesha Indians with the support of the World Wide Fund for Nature.

A representative puts the case this way: 'When we want to manage the forest ourselves, we simply need to IMITATE NATURE, and in that way we will always have forest. The management plan consists of harvesting all the trees in the form of NARROW STRIPS. These strips are normally 20 metres wide by 500 or more metres long. From a strip of this size one can harvest more or less 85,000 board feet of cylindrical wood of various sizes and different species. The large trees which are in the forest around the strip will cast their seeds and in this way produce new young plants in order to recuperate this artificial new opening. In this way the strip will be repopulated or reforested by nature itself. The owner of the forest will need only to respect the law of nature; he will not have to 'sow' any trees. Nature does all the work. After 40 years the same strip will be ready to be harvested again.

DEFORESTATION: TIMBER & DEVELOPMENT

The most obvious source of revenue from tropical forests is timber. Felling trees for their wood is known as logging. The total trade from selling hardwoods overseas comes to some £6 billion each year. This timber is beautiful, long lasting and much sought after – demand is growing fast around the world. Each year, some 5 million hectares of tropical forests are cut for timber and related products, including paper pulp.

Forest loss for this purpose is at its greatest in West Africa and Asia and is gaining momentum in the Amazon forests of South America. The economics of the issue are related to the great debts which developing countries owe to foreign nations and international banks. The governments in debt are understandably very keen to export timber at a high

Felling and removing just one tree can cause widespread damage

price and obtain foreign currency in return. This is a way of deriving instant benefit from resources that appear to be plentiful and in world demand.

Over half of all tropical hardwood timber cut is exported. The leading importer is Japan, which takes in some 40 per cent of the world's total exports. The USA is the second largest consumer. Because of this ever-increasing demand major exporters of hardwoods like the Philippines may not have sufficient timber for their own domestic markets within the next decade.

A great deal of wood is also used for fuel purposes. Timber is an industrial fuel in many tropical countries and as industries develop, so does their fuel requirement. In Brazil, for example, the steel industry based on local iron ore deposits is expanding rapidly, necessitating thousands of hectares of forest loss. Wood is also the main source of energy for almost 90 per cent of people in developing lands. Cooking and heating depend on it, and the removal of trees for this purpose makes no small impact on the overall problem.

A final area for concern is the use of wood for paper. Until recently, good quality hardwoods were not channelled in this direction, but new and 'progressive' techniques now enable industry to convert hardwoods into paper pulp. One example from Japan is of a company that manufactures paper packaging from timber imported from the rainforests of Papua New Guinea.

Major advances have been made in logging techniques. Whilst traditionally it may have taken a group of men an entire day to cut

down one tree with axes, one labourer can now fell a tree in a matter of minutes with the aid of a chain-saw. Modern machinery is capable of reducing a whole tree to tiny chips of wood in seconds. This sounds like progress, yet, quite apart from the impact of direct deforestation of trees, there is an indirect problem caused by careless methods and negligence. One felled tree often means damage to many others: there may be only two or three trees suitable for logging in a certain area. Imagine the scene when one colossal tree comes crashing down amongst its

neighbours. This, together with the heavy equipment needed as it is felled and dragged away through the forest, will inevitably 'bruise' and damage many other trees and plants. Think also of the effect on bird and animal life, which will inevitably disappear or be destroyed as large machines move in. It is estimated that in a given patch of forest, when one tree is felled, two-thirds of other living things will be damaged or destroyed.

Negligence may also lead to extensive forest fires. In Borneo in 1983, for example, insufficient

care taken in logging practices was in part responsible for a major forest fire that burned for four months. A huge area was destroyed, which obviously included trees and other valuable forest plants, animals, birds and insects.

Another major direct cause of deforestation is large-scale development projects. These include the clearance of land and sale of wood to make space for roads, dams, industrial sites and housing. Many such projects achieve little or no success, whilst causing major damage to forests. In Brazil, for example, large-scale pro-grammes designed to encourage people to colonize and develop have been blamed for the loss of over 25 per cent of the Amazonian forests in a ten year period.

So far this seems a picture of doom and gloom. Fortunately, there are examples of excellent practice in the timber industry (look at page 37). In this co-operative in Peru, efforts are being made to manage the removal of timber in such a way that it will not result in permanent loss. There is another example of good management, this time in Malaysia, on page 52.

Huge trees in Gabon are felled in minutes and transported in large numbers by truck

DEFORESTATION: CATTLE RANCHING

Every year some 8 million hectares of rainforest are cleared for cultivation or the growing of crops. Most of this land is used for the type of farming employed by people whose home is the forest, and known as shifting cultivation or 'slash and burn' agriculture. This is an ancient and long-established method that is successful for the growing of crops.

During the time it takes you to read this book, thousands of acres of forest land will be destroyed. Much of this destruction is for large-scale agriculture. When trees are cleared away, the earth will soon dry out and become unusable

Turning forests into burgers (right)

A family clears a small plot in the forest by slashing or cutting down the vegetation which is then burned, allowing the bonfire ashes to add fertility to the poor-quality soil. Crops such as vegetables and grains will then be grown on that plot for two or three years, or until all of the nutrients in the soil have been used up.

The farming family then moves on to another patch of forest which is cleared and cultivated while the original plot rests and slowly builds up its store of plant nutrients. In order to do this, it will need to go back to its wild, natural state and may lie unused (fallow) for up to 30 years before a farmer returns to it. Within months of being abandoned, forest plants will begin to return to the used patch. This is called secondary growth and takes place very quickly in the hot, moist atmosphere. A mass of vegetation five metres tall could well be established in only five years, and within ten years there will be tall young trees. It is the falling of leaves and decomposition from this vegetation that gradually builds up the fertility of the soil.

Traditionally, this slash and burn method of farming has worked and the forest has naturally renewed itself. Today, however, the situation is different. A much higher population density makes forest clearing much more frequent and extensive, and new methods are being introduced. Even with the traditional system, as more mature trees are removed, there are not enough tree seeds to fall on the abandoned plot to provide an adequate range of seedlings for the new secondary forest. Renewal is therefore failing. Also, with increasing pressure on availability of land, soils are rested for much shorter periods or not rested at all. Fertility is lost, and cleared plots are left exposed to soil erosion and loss of even more nutrients from rainfall. Eventually all that remains is an agricultural wasteland.

Adding to this gloomy picture is the fact that vegetation is now sometimes cleared by tractors rather than by hand. This causes new tree growth to be slower, adding to the likelihood of exposure of bare land to storms and soil erosion. It is estimated that current misuse of land in this way is responsible for 50 per cent of tropical deforestation in Asia and as much as 70 per cent in Africa. It is a perfect example of how 'progress' and new farming methods have destroyed a traditional system that was in harmony with the ecosystem.

A traditional method of agriculture. Peasant farmers in Togo build earth mounds to control soil erosion, then plant yams in them. The tubers have loose soil to grow in, but the heavy rainfall does not flood the crop

To turn to farming on a much larger scale, land clearing for cattle production causes very extensive destruction of forests, particularly in Latin America. There, it has been claimed, cattle ranching is 'turning forests into hamburgers'.

More than 25 per cent of this region's rainforest has been cut down and turned over to grassland in the last 25 years. Cattle which graze on these pastures produce the beef which supplies the USA with countless millions of burgers. The economic incentives are great. Beef from Central America is available at a lower cost than that produced within the USA. Since 1960, one-third of Costa Rica's rainforest area has been cut for grazing land, ranches have increased greatly in size and export figures for beef have multiplied by seven.

Once it has been cleared for cattle ranching, the land is productive for only a short time. Soil erosion and nutrient depletion is inevitable. Continued pressure on the ground from vehicles and the hooves of cattle only makes the problem worse. A vicious circle is created – the useless land is abandoned, more forest is cleared by the cattle ranchers and so on. It is possible that more efficient farming methods could break into this cycle and help to preserve the land. Unfortunately, it is often the case that government incentives together with 'help' from aid agencies on an international basis actually encourage and support extensive cattle ranching so that beef can be reared for export.

Erosion on deforested land in the Amazon (above right)

1 hamburger

sq.m. of forest - the size of a room

SLOWING DEFORESTATION

It is vital for many reasons that ways are found to slow tropical deforestation. It may seem understandable and excusable that rainforests are destroyed in order to allow for economic growth and expansion in developing lands, yet when a tropical forest is removed, an entire ecosystem is destroyed, with incredibly far-reaching consequences.

By the year 2000 it is likely that **up to a million plant and animal species will have been eliminated from the world.** Less than 5 per cent of forests have any kind of legislation for protecting wildlife so extinctions seem inevitable.

If the trees of the rainforest disappear, the soil, water cycle and climate will all be affected

This wild melon has been used as a medicine for hundreds of years by local dwellers in the forests of Belize. Scientists are now investigating its value for treating a number of diseases (far right)

One source describes this scenario as a biological holocaust, the consequences of which are devastating. Even if reversal were possible, it would take millions of years for life on earth to re-establish its rich diversity.

A second major consequence is the **displacement of traditional cultures.** For thousands of years, tribes followed ways of life that allowed them to live in harmony with the natural world. As tropical lands are destroyed, established cultures and vast knowledge of forest ecology will be eliminated too. The quality of life for such displaced people is also likely to take a dramatic turn for the worse. They may be forced into reservations or into new and unwanted lifestyles, for example, as low-paid labourers. Those who refuse to leave their traditional homes may even be killed.

Thirdly, forest loss is **devastating to soils, water and climate.** Soil erosion is a real and serious threat, alongside silting of waterways and flooding. Tropical forests moderate their local climates by heating and cooling the air, maintaining humidity and condensation. Furthermore, tropical forests may have a fundamental role in the world-wide climate and their destruction is known to contribute to the well-documented 'Greenhouse Effect' which causes global warming and rising sea levels.

The fourth area of consequences concerns the **loss of valuable products** from the world. Agricultural, industrial and medicinal goods will inevitably become scarce as more and more trees are destroyed. Furthermore, if deforestation continues, the potential for identifying new useful plants

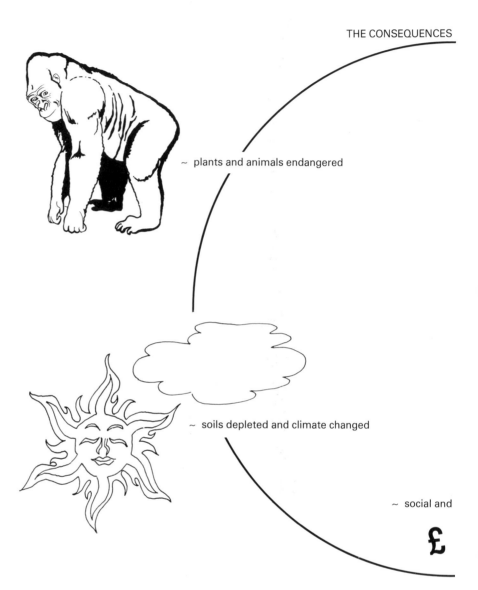

THE CONSEQUENCES

~ plants and animals endangered

~ soils depleted and climate changed

~ social and

£

and chemicals which may be derived from them is obviously curtailed.

The combination of these losses and consequences in turn contribute to a **wide range of economic, social and political problems.** Millions of people have left traditional homes in Central America and elsewhere to escape poverty, diminishing water and food supplies and degraded soils. Such people can no longer support themselves. Deforestation leads to environmental deterioration, poverty and inevitable conflicts. It may lead to political instability or even war.

In total, the consequences of tropical deforestation are incalculable. Perhaps in an ideal world, the felling of tropical trees would suddenly stop, but, to be realistic, the major trend needs to be a dramatic slowing down of deforestation rates. Key questions

OF DEFORESTATION

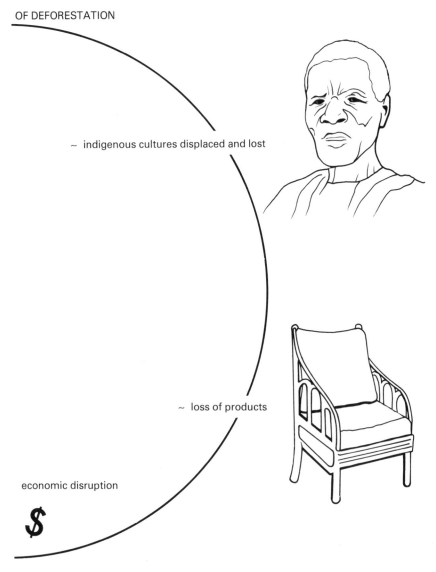

~ indigenous cultures displaced and lost

~ loss of products

economic disruption

$

Slowing deforestation may be achieved by a 7-fold integrated plan:
- establishing reserves in forests
- improving management
- preventing large development projects
- restoration of land
- slowing population growth
- improving agriculture
- slowing down the demand for products

for conservation include: How much of the world's forest lands can now be saved? How may destruction rates be reduced? Can the forests be conserved and sensibly used at the same time? What methods can be used to protect the forests?

And, last but not least, who should take action?

Efforts to slow and reverse deforestation rates include the establishment of special forest reserves to protect land and species. They also include the improvement of forest management, preventing large-scale development projects that destroy resources, restoring deforested land, slowing population growth, improving agricultural practices and slowing down the demand for forest products.

NATURE RESERVES & TIMBER MANAGEMENT

The establishment of specially protected national parks and nature reserves is essential if forests are to be conserved. They are places where species are protected, tourism and research are encouraged and certain activities such as agriculture, logging, hunting, road-building and industry are banned. In the world as a whole, less than 5 per cent of remaining forests are protected as parks or reserves. Brazil has an established system of conservation areas that cover almost 15 million hectares and in Costa Rica a mixture of parks, wildlife refuges and Indian reserves protect 80 per cent of the remaining forest lands.

These are impressive attempts, but are not without many problems. Often there are too few rangers to manage and patrol the areas and enforce the rules. Also, whilst originally established in remote places that were almost inaccessible, the parks and reserves are now becoming much easier to reach. Roads and airstrips are being constructed close by. Helpful as these features may be for tourists and researchers, they also spell trouble in the form of poachers, illegal settlers, possibilities for smuggling out valuable hardwood logs and the illegal selling of animals and skins to traders.

The Mountain Pine Ridge in the highlands of Belize has been set aside as a forest reserve. It is hoped to preserve the Caribbean Pine as a tree species and use it in a sustainable way

The jaguar is one of many animal and plant species which are protected from widescale habitat depletion and hunting within the 400 square km of the Cockscomb Forest Jaguar Preserve in Belize

It is not within the capability of many governments to manage these areas effectively — they simply do not have the experience, expertise, people and money necessary for successful administration. In order for national parks and reserves to be successful, the government in question must firmly believe in and support the idea. Part of this commitment involves the elimination of exploitation and illegal practices by providing opportunities for activities to happen elsewhere, for example, setting aside routes for roads, and allowing logging, farming and mining in other specified locations.

Research has shown that in those reserves which are successful in their conservation attempts, local people have been totally involved in both planning and management. Also, successful reserves are those which have been designed to benefit people as well as natural resources. A typical reserve of this kind has distinct

SKS/Simmah Timber Industries
A case study of good practice

A highly successful method of achieving sustainable production has been developed by SKS/Simmah Timber Industries, a partly British-owned company based in Malaysia. Their solution lies in making use of the massive amount of hardwood which is usually wasted. It is estimated that conventional logging and manufacturing processes result in up to 45 per cent wastage of the timber harvested. SKS/Simmah use a 'pre-cycling process', in which otherwise waste hardwood is put to good use. Narrow diameter sections of wood are retained, sliced into layers, and compressed to form ply-hardwood sections. These sections are then compressed to form a solid core of hardwood which is strong, heavy, durable and can constitute 70 per cent of a final timber product. There are three key advantages to this system:

- the customer gets a stronger product that costs no more than its conventionally manufactured counterpart;
- the economy of the timber producer does not suffer. In fact, employment increases;
- most importantly of all, deforestation through logging is slowed to a rate at which sustainability, through natural regrowth and programmed replanting, becomes demonstrably feasible.

SKS/Simmah Timber Industries use narrow pieces of timber that would otherwise be wasted. The process requires a lot of labour and a larger than average workforce is employed — including women, which is unusual in the timber industry

Key issues in conservation management

Knowledge of forest ecosystems is essential. This will help governments to plan carefully and give effective control.

Considering alternatives. Before any mature primary rainforest is destroyed, alternatives should be considered. Perhaps there are secondary forests or already disturbed areas that could be used for agriculture, mining, and the building of roads and towns so that primaries are protected.

Speed and size. Very large-scale development schemes should be avoided. Their efforts are devastating. They can easily get out of control and have 'knock-on' effects that were never planned. Moving ahead too fast is a similar problem. Time should be allowed to consider the overall and long-term effects of development.

Skills should be used wisely. Local indigenous people have a vast range of forest skills that have been employed for years without harming the ecosystem.

Natural systems can teach us so much. For thousands of years, local tribes lived in harmony with the natural world. The forest is a highly successful ecosystem when left alone. Developments should imitate the natural forest and its layers. The system as a whole should be maintained.

ZONES OF A SUCCESSFUL FOREST

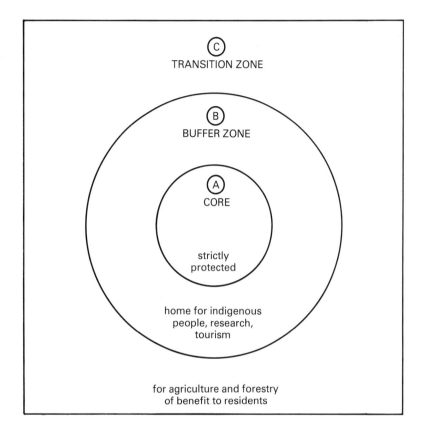

zones. In the centre is a core of strictly protected land (no dwelling, agriculture, logging, mining or developments). Around this is a 'buffer zone' for low-density inhabitation by local people and activities such as research, tourism and education. Beyond this is a 'transition zone' in which agriculture and forestry take place – providing food and income for the reserve dwellers.

The Malaysian government takes the problem of deforestation very seriously. The country's forests are home to 14,500 species of flowering plants, well over 200 species of mammals, 600 species of birds, 140 species of snakes, 150 species of frogs and thousands of species of insects. To avoid drastic depletion of the forests, Malaysia has established policies

and plans to manage them as a renewable resource. The forestry and timber industries play a major role in the socio-economic life of Malaysia, so the government needs to balance ecological conservation and economic development. Several strategies have been adopted to achieve this, including:

• limiting the export of timber and forest produce in their 'raw' forms;
• promoting better use of a wider range of timber species to reduce wastage;
• rationalizing the annual allowable cut from natural forest to ensure sustainable management;
• promoting the use of timber from tree crops other than those from the natural forest.

GLOBAL ACTION

Management, restoration and progress can be approached at a variety of levels and no-one would disagree with the fact that large organizations, governments and international agencies have a key role to play. The good news is that there *is* considerable evidence of progress at global level to slow deforestation. In 1984 an American study reviewed priorities for action and proposed a ten year global programme of funding to take account of four key areas:

• establishing a much wider network of well-managed national reserves and parks;
• expanding tree plantations and reafforestation programmes;
• expanding research programmes and management training;
• developing improved facilities for processing hardwoods in their native lands.

Red Colobus monkey (above)
Devastated forest (background)

Funding for this proposal was planned to come from the governments of developing countries, private sources such as timber corporations, and taxes on imported hardwood products.

In 1985 a worldwide Tropical Forestry Action Plan was developed by the United Nations Food and Agriculture Organization, the World Resources Institute, other non-governmental organizations and agencies and representatives from over 60 nations around the world. Once again, this plan focuses on action areas, namely:

• the integration of forestry and agriculture so that land may be used in a 'sustainable' way – that is, resources will not be destroyed but will be renewed;
• development of forest industries that are also sustainable – that is, they will not remove valuable resources for ever;
• conservation of fuelwood and the development of new fuel resources;
• conservation of tropical forest ecosystems;
• developing, planning, research and education.

Within the overall framework provided by this internationally supported, though controversial, Forest Action Plan, agencies concerned with development are co-ordinating loans and grants, and many countries are implementing national action plans. Initially the plan received widespread support from both governmental and non-governmental organizations. It has since been the subject of fierce criticism and controversy. In 1987, the World Rainforest Movement (consisting of major Third World and Western environmental groups), together with *The Ecologist* journal, proposed an alternative plan. This identifies four key interrelated components that need to be changed: ending the debt crisis; reforming trade patterns; halting environmentally destructive development projects; and land ownership reform. This revised plan is intended to be a framework for discussion.

Throughout the world therefore there has been a recent and dramatic increase in the efforts of environmental and other non-governmental organizations, industries and the media to aid the conservation of rainforests. Conservation organizations such as the World Wide Fund for Nature (WWF) and Friends of the Earth have mounted massive campaigns aimed at increasing public awareness of what is happening to tropical forests. Some of these campaigns are of a general 'Save The Rainforests' nature, whilst others are aimed at conserving particular areas or endangered species – such as 'Save The Gorilla'.

A final point of interest to consider is the withholding of cash as well as the donation of it.

Loading timber onto a lorry in Brazil

Building a railway through the Brazilian Amazon

Industrial companies and other organizations are doing their share of the action for conservation.

For example:

Coca-Cola
has donated land for a reserve in Central America

Midland Bank
contributes towards maintaining a National Park in Cameroon

Fiat
sponsored a WWF initiative concerned with the protection of lemurs in Madagascar

Jaguar Car Company
maintains reserves (and jaguars!) in South America

Rich countries and organizations can have a tremendous impact on the fate of the forests. Besides giving money for worthwhile conservation and development schemes that will actually benefit the rainforests, they may also withhold cash from projects which damage these ecosystems. Much criticism has been levelled at the World Bank which has put a lot of money into large-scale development projects. As a result, payments for a road project in Brazil that was having adverse effects on both the rainforest environment and on the Indians who lived there were stopped, and the government was required to rethink its development projects in the Amazon area. Government policy certainly can be changed if enough pressure is applied, and action taken.

IS THERE A ROLE FOR THE INDIVIDUAL?

Every individual can make a contribution – no matter how small – towards the vital task of preserving the rainforests of the world. We can change our lifestyle . . .

. . . they cannot change theirs

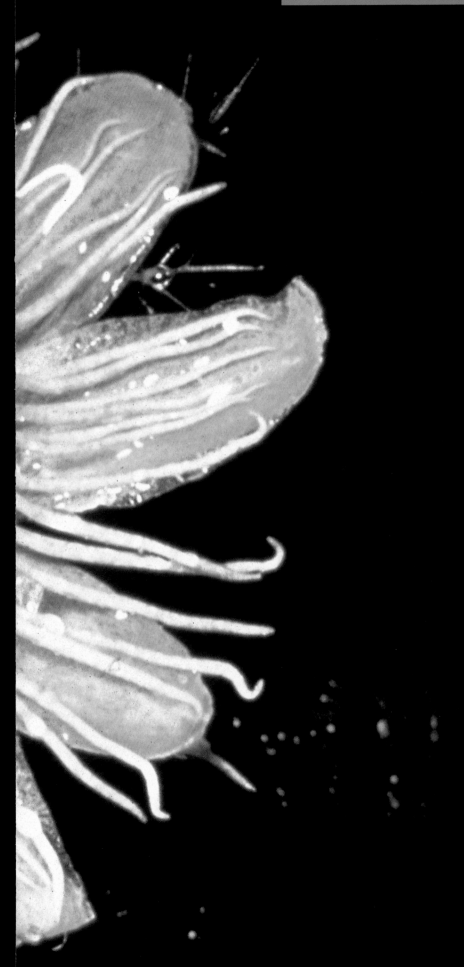

What an important question this is. Is the problem of rainforest conservation too complex, too vast and too expensive to warrant an individual's attention and action? The answer is a resounding NO! Every one of us can help to save the forests. Indeed, it could be argued that practical, small-scale initiatives may actually be more successful than major international conferences. Whilst we may not have such an influential impact upon the world of the rain forests as an individual like Chico Mendes (see next page), each of us can take action in a host of simple yet effective ways. We can help by joining with others and by thinking carefully about our habits and lifestyles.

Change your habits and lifestyle

So much devastation of rain forests is a direct result of world demands for forest goods.

- Encourage your family and friends not to buy furniture or other products that have been made from tropical hardwoods such as mahogany and teak unless they have derived from sustainable timber management.
- Ask timber and furniture store owners where their tropical products have come from. Even if they do not know, this helps to raise awareness and perhaps persuade them to think carefully about their goods. If enough people refuse to buy them, action would have to be taken.
- Try to find out where your hamburger meat comes from and, if it is from a tropical country, raise the issue with the supplier.
- Do not keep a tropical animal or plant unless you are certain that it was born/grown in your own country.
- Take an active part in community conservation programmes. These might include recycling schemes. If paper is recycled and put to good further use, then this will reduce the demand for new paper from the world's trees.

Some of these actions may appear to be on a very small scale, but together they may have a significant impact.

Join together

- Talk with friends, relatives and teachers about the issues and try to persuade them to join in the action. Do some further reading and find out as much as you can about the complexities of the causes and consequences of deforestation. Knowledge and understanding go a long way towards solving problems.
- Join an international conservation organization such as the World Wide Fund for Nature (WWF) or Friends of the Earth (useful addresses are on page 63). Quite apart from helping with funds, by joining with others in this way, you will have the chance to learn a great deal more about conservation, work on exciting projects and meet new people who share your interests and concerns.
- Donate some money, if you are in a position to do so. Every tiny donation helps to swell much-needed funds.
- Get together with friends to organize a fund-raising event.
- Write to your Member of Parliament and other government ministers. Urge them to adopt policies that are aimed at protecting rainforests and developing a sustainable future for developing countries. It is unlikely that any government will make this a top priority unless enough people join in the persuasion.

In many areas it is already too late to save the rainforests. It is vital that this depressing fact does not deter the world from taking action. So much can still be achieved in other places. Consider the following statement, taken from the publicity material of the charity, Earthlife:

In the time it will take you to read this page, 100 acres of tropical rainforest will be destroyed. Every minute of every day, the cutting, burning and bulldozing continues.

At this rate, the forests – the oldest and richest expressions of life on the planet – will all be gone within 40 years. Our generation will have presided over the greatest extinction of living things since the ecological catastrophe that wiped out the dinosaurs.

This biological holocaust is burning great holes in the web of life that sustains us all . . .

The issue is indeed of concern to us all. Each and every one of us can take specific action. Furthermore, we can consider fundamental ways in which people may move towards living in harmony with the natural world, forming an integral part of the environment rather than exploiting it.

Chico Mendes ... the ultimate sacrifice

Francisco Alves Mendes Filho – or Chico Mendes – died on 22 December 1988. He was assassinated in the Brazilian Amazon. The story of Chico's death is now well known throughout the world. He was an individual who cared, and who paid the ultimate sacrifice for attempting to defend the rainforests of the Amazon. Chico led a movement which brought together the poor people of the forest who had been expelled from their homes and which aimed to save the Amazon from deforestation and illegal logging. With other local union leaders, he founded the National Council of Rubber Tappers, which aims to create co-operatives and organize forest communities. Its members wish to have the freedom to organize themselves and their alliances freely, to participate in public decisions and challenge the local elite with its 'power, money and guns'.

Chico was one of a thousand rural union leaders, Indians and their supporters killed in Brazil since 1980. As such local efforts to protect the native land increased, so too did violence against activists and leaders. Most of these murders took place in the Amazon area. All leaders of the National Council of Rubber Tappers have received death threats. It is reported that there is evidence of the involvement of local landowners and government officials in Chico's murder. Such reports have brought no charges.

Chico's great legacy includes a greatly increased awareness of the needs and concerns of rubber tappers and their allies – the indigenous groups – which is now receiving powerful political support in Brazil.

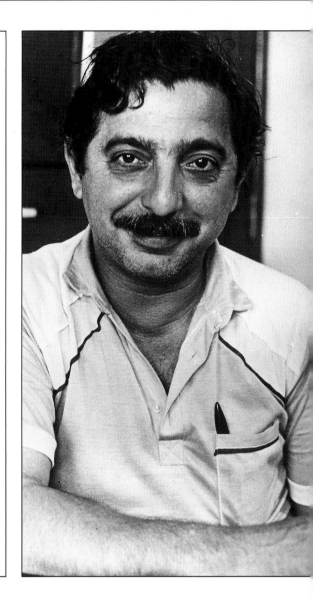

GLOSSARY

Adaptation
The way living things change their form and way of life to suit their environmental conditions.

Chlorophyll
Green pigment found in plants.

Decomposition
The breakdown of dead animal and plant life into simpler substances.

Ecosystem
An assembly of organisms which interact with each other, together with the environment in which they live.

Extinct
Died out.

Hardwood
A wood whose tissues are tightly packed together.

Holocaust
Wholesale killing and destruction.

Invertebrates
Animals without backbones.

Leaching
The dissolving and removal of substances in the soil by water.

Niche
The place a plant or animal occupies in the ecosystem.

Nutrients
Plant food in the soil. Inorganic nutrients are from minerals in the earth's rocks. Organic nutrients are from decaying organisms.

Photosynthesis
The making of organic substances in plants from water and carbon dioxide. The energy used is the sunlight captured by chlorophyll.

Pollination
The fertilization of a flower by carrying pollen to the pistil.

Shifting cultivation
'slash and burn'
Names for a type of farming where a patch of land is cleared, crops are grown for 2–3 years, then the patch is abandoned for a number of years so that it can regain its fertility.

Species
A category in the classification of animals and plants. Individuals within a species breed successfully.

RESOURCES & ADDRESSES

Earthlife
10 Belgrave Square
LONDON
SW1X 8PH

Friends of the Earth Trust Ltd
26–28 Underwood Street
LONDON
N1 7JQ

Greenpeace (UK)
Canonbury Villas
LONDON
N1 2PN

Greenpeace (USA)
1611 Connecticut Avenue NW
Washington DC
2009

Rainforest Action Network (USA)
301 Broadway; Suite A
San Francisco
CA 94133

World Wide Fund for Nature (UK)
Panda House
Weyside Park
Godalming
Surrey
GV7 1QU

World Wide Fund for Nature (USA)
1250 24th Street NW
Washington DC
20037

INDEX